Eels
DISCOVER

Thanks for checking out the DISCOVER Books Series. Please note: All Rights Reserved. No part of this publication may be reproduced in any form or by any means, including scanning, photocopying, or otherwise without prior written permission of the copyright holder. Copyright © 2014

Eels

Eels are a very odd and a very cool creature. Eels are a type of fish. There are around 800 different species of the Eel. This type of sea critter is eaten a lot by people in Japan. In this book we are going to explore the world of the Eel. We will learn stuff like where it lives, what it eats and what special ability the Eel has. So read on to discover and to learn more about this slippery critter.

Where in the World?

Did you know the Eel can be found in most waters around the world? Eels can live in freshwater or saltwater. Though, they do prefer to live in shallower water. They will keep hidden in holes called, Eel pits. These are found at the bottom of the ocean or water source.

The Body of the Eel

Did you know the body of the Eel is snake-like? Eels have long bodies that are more flat than a snake. They do not have single fins on the bottom of their bodies. In fact, their top and bottom fins are fused along the body of the Eel. This forms a ribbon along the length of the Eel.

The Size of an Eel

Did you know the Eel can range in size? Eels can be very small. These little guys only weigh about 1.1 ounce (30 grams). Some larger species can reach lengths of 5 to 13 feet long (1.5 to 3.9 meters). These big Eels can weigh around 55 pounds (25 kilograms).

The Skin of an Eel

Did you know Eels have a special covering on their skin? Eels are covered with a slimy coating. This allows them to slither along the bottom of the ocean and around the coral and stones without getting harmed. Unlike fish, they do not have any scales and their skin is smooth to the touch.

The Senses of the Eel

Did you know the Eel has poor eyesight? In fact, some divers have been bitten by an Eel because they think fingers are food. Eels have a strong sense of touch and smell. Some Eels can feel the movement given off other sea creatures. Other Eels have an acute sense of hearing. This helps them hunt for prey.

What the Eel Eats

Did you know Eels have a huge appetite? Eels are carnivores. This means they only eat meat. They will dine on fish, lobsters, octopuses, snails, crabs, mussels and frogs. They have very strong jaws and sharp pointy teeth. The Eel will stay hidden in its hole, then pop out and grab its prey.

What Eats the Eel

Did you know people hunt and eat Eels? People have hunted the Eel for food for many years. They are considered a delicacy in some cultures. The Eels natural predators are large fish, seabirds, raccoons, crocodiles and other large mammals. Some Eels do not have any predators because of their size.

How the Eel Moves

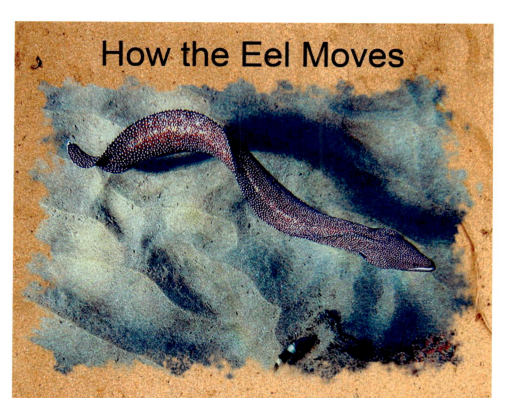

Did you know Eels can swim backwards and forwards? Eels move in the water in an undulated motion. This is like how a rollercoaster moves. Eels can also travel for short distances on land. Most Eels rest during the day and hunt for food at night. This makes them nocturnal.

Adult Eels

Did you know the adult Eels have a special courting ritual? A male and female Eel will open their mouths really wide. They will then wrap their bodies around each other. This can go on for hours. They will separate after the female has laid her eggs. The male then fertilizes the eggs.

Female Eels

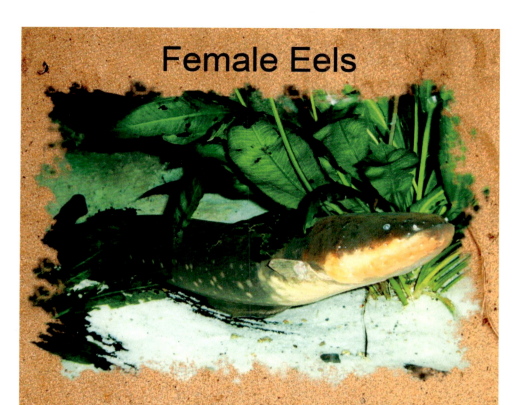

Did you know some female Eels do not mate until they are very old? Female Eels live longer than the male Eels do. Some species of female Eels breed when they are from 60 to 100 years old! The female will release her eggs. Once they have been fertilized they drift off in the ocean currents.

Baby Eels

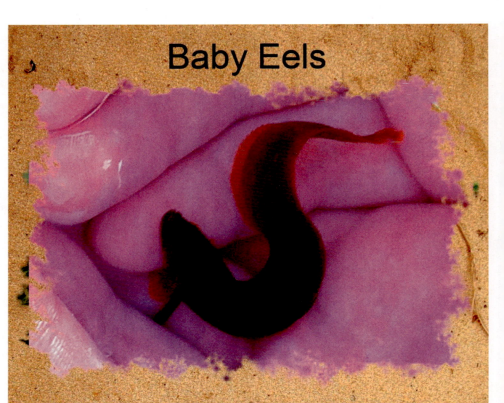

Did you know the larvae stage of the baby Eel eats marine snow? This is small particles of food and debris that floats in the water. Baby eels are called 'elvers'. The eels go through a larval phase as juveniles and form part of the plankton.

Life of the Eel

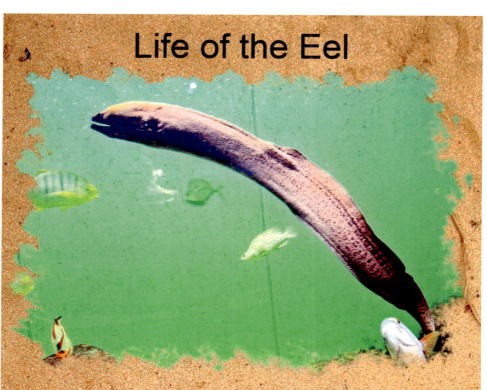

Did you know the Eel can live for a very long time? Healthy Eels can have a lifespan of about 100 years-old. You can see some species of Eels at marine exhibits or in the ocean (if you are really lucky). After most Eels mate, they die and let the young ones take over.

The Electric Eel

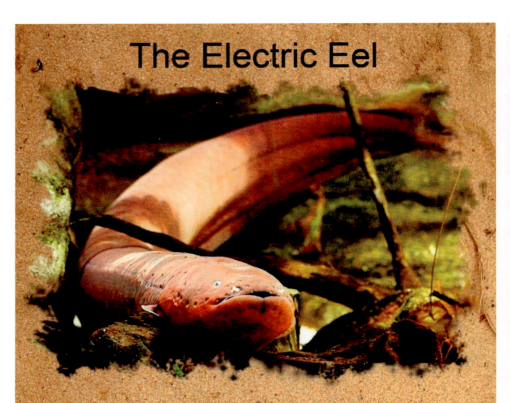

Did you know the Electric Eel is not really an Eel? This creature is more closely related to the carp and catfish. Electric Eels can grow to be around 6 feet long (2 meters). They can weigh up to 44 pounds (20 kilograms). This Eel is well known for giving off a high voltage shock.

The Moray Eel

Did you know the Moray Eel is feared by many people? There is around 200 different species of this Eel The Moray Eel has a big mouth with many long sharp canine teeth. It can even wrap itself into a knot to anchor itself when it is tearing into its food.

Quiz

Question 1: Where are Eels found?

Answer 1: In saltwater and in freshwater

Question 2: What is the skin of an Eel covered in?

Answer 2: A slimy coating

Question 3: What are the holes that Eels live in called?

Answer 3: Eel Pits

Question 4: How does the Eel move?

Answer 4: Forwards and backwards in an undulated motion

Question 5: What is marine snow?

Answer 5: The tiny particles of food that the Eel larvae

Thank you for checking out another title from DISCOVER Books! Make sure to check out Amazon.com for many other great books.

Made in the USA
San Bernardino, CA
26 February 2019